Of This Too

Of This Too

Poems by Celia Merlin

Terrace Top Press
Tel Aviv

Poetry

Book and cover design: Jacob Palm

Acknowledgments

Spanning decades and continents, it is here that I would like to deeply thank the many people who have helped me now and over the years.

To Michael Dickel, my multi-talented editor and friend for all his help, patience and knowledge. To author/poet, Shawn Edrei, for offering his expertise, having my back, and keeping me on track and still smiling when I detoured. To the many people at Voices Israel, who provided a home for my voice in a strange land.

To my parents, who have always listened, advised and encouraged from early on. To my many teachers who inspired and challenged. To my dear friend Julie Schreiber Yosefyan, and all the friends and loved ones who were bombarded with unanswerable, trick questions. To my children, Oren, Yoni, and Shani along with my husband, Yechiel- you have embraced this strange, odd part of me and have always shown me the understanding and support to start, stop, start, stop and start again. To my wonderful sisters, Perrie, Rae and VeeVee- the journey has always been with and so much about you.

I would like to thank the editors of the following journals for including these poems or earlier versions in their collections:

Voices Israel: "Teeth," "Aliyah—The Language," "Harvesting," "Virtual Snub," "Lightning Bugs," "Piano at Night," "Spin and Sing," "Overwhelming Wonder," "Trip to the Theatre," "At the Airport," "Big Kids," "Paris Unsaid," "The Field, Lexington KY, 1961,""Fur," "Whirlpool—For Shani," "Reconciliation," " In the Flaw," "Borders," "Celia Merlin," "Eliyahu in the Skies," "Watching for VeeVee Part II Gulf War," "Ozymandias Revisited"ARC, *Journal of the Israel Association of Writers in English*: "Full Frontal," "American Tu B'Shvat—Nuts," "Tel Aviv Beach—Winter Abundance," "For a Second"*The Last Stanza—An Anthology of Poems from Tel Aviv*: "Jewish Christmas—Buffalo, New York," "Ghost of Thanksgiving Past," "Israeli Fall," "Minor Misunderstanding," "Entitlement and Myths about Pink Cotton Panties"*Muddy River Poetry Review*: "Remote Control," "A Certain Risk," "Yet in Sight"

ISBN   978-965-572-306-9

Terrace Top Press
Tel Aviv

To my Mom and Dad,
Ruthie and Yatz Merlin

of words   of words   of words   1

of   hearth   and   home   13

of   that   which   is   around   31

of words   *of words*   *of words*

Aliyah—The Language

I came here bringing
pumpkin and squash,
starched autumn air,
clay, dark and oozing
fat clouds,
and snow,
all in a basket, familiar and safe
in color and nuance.

I found here
yellow and hamsin,
turquoise and froth,
irises, cacti and gardens of granite
speaking to me in tongues.

Ten summers have passed
and I haven't forgotten
cut grass in my toes or
the firefly's glow, summer thunder and steam.

But jasmine heat climbs to my terrace now
and mint sweats sweet in my tea,
and the orange blossoms beckon,
singing welcome: come touch.

And at last
I have opened my arms.

Teeth

"You grind your teeth,"
the dentist tells me.
And from that day on
I notice it's true—

I grind my teeth
not only at night, but
on the bus, at work,

as I dunk the little children
in their bath,
little onion heads.

I grind my teeth and I don't know
if this was always true
and unnoticed
or if new and intensifying.

I churn my teeth and
like butter they bend
yellow-white on red gums.

Tin foil fillings—
rejected transplants in spaces emptied.
Foreign.

Whose mouth is this that exudes such force?
What words are those being ground to a pulp?

Dinner Party—Paris

The lilies were wet when I bought them,
my black skirt slightly damp against my thigh.

Mine is the ninth Kir on the table. Its cassis
mixes light with white wine. From the corners, Joni plays,
singing: "Help me, I think I'm falling..." —lamb moist, talk
rapid and alive. I like your guests. They take turns passing
jokes across a blue linen cloth and
I miss my cue more than once.

My hair, too tight; my shirt, too stiff;
their laughter, healthy and full.
I butt my cigarette and try hard to think of something
clever. Passé composé, L'imparfait, maybe tu? Maybe vous?

My eyes are on the lilies, my skirt slightly damp against my thigh.
To the sounds and motions of people I don't know,
tonight I remember only words.

Full Frontal

You stand behind
your too
naked words.
Convenient camouflage,

a spot light
angled white
on your face,
tricking us into thinking
we really see.

But their nakedness—

as if revealing,
as if forthright,
with no one to claim
they're the Emperor's
New Clothes,

allowing us to view
full frontal and raw

the best sleight of hand
of all.

Harvesting

Overwhelmed by the beauty
of other peoples' words,
I am numbed by the noise
in my head.

Idea to idea
picture to picture
must be whittled down
from tree to stick to
perfect flute
to raw to gut and true.

How can I work when
characters crowd
and letters leap out,
when dusks are devoured
or drip through cheesecloth,
when moss stains nostrils
and goats go grazing

in phrases I wish that
I had birthed, that
I had dug up
first?

People You May Know

Scrolling Facebook your face
keeps appearing—
people you may know—
many times. With your right
arm resting above your head,
an unusual pose, at that.

Between weekend vodkas, I imagine
your story—the one you've sent out,
eyes straight on, fluorescent tulips,
they stop me or anyone else
you may know.

As in bed, on a pillow, your arm
on your head, lays spent, post-sex
cigarette, though we both have quit.

Between weekend drinks, I see
ten common friends,
and some are museums or businesses,
only one, maybe two know my name.

And I don't know if
you are married or
single or complicated.
So complicated.

Your right arm rests on your head and the lens
loves you and so do you so sexy,
your likes show desire for ideas I love.

And you could be gay,
for all I know—there's a pose in one picture
where I think it's so—on an armchair, both legs
to the side and you're leaning.

But there are also some kids in the pictures
you share, who share
your last name, and your arm
hugs them warmly, same arm from the photo of
the you I may know, and you
all are so happy and handsome and close.

And I wonder- where's "Mom"? Though
I'm happily married.
Is she taking the picture? Off on a spree
with her new beloved on a tropical isle?

Or is she holding a grudge, this very same moment
I'm scanning the life of the you that you've shared,
for the years that she's lost with your arm on your head,
for the life you've created for someone like me,

after two weekend vodkas, just scrolling
on Facebook through people that
I may know.

Virtual Snub

It started when she liked my status
and I didn't like her back.
It wasn't that I didn't like her.
Perhaps I missed or overlooked it
(or I didn't like that others would see
that I liked her like).
But that's when it started.

Once I liked someone else's like
and she made a comment.
But not to me. I was not included.
Just heard the ting-ting every time
someone wrote, and me
overlooked.

And since, I see her liking all others—
some liking back, some not.

And that damn
ticker thingy on the side
keeps on rolling with
liking and tagging and
comments and more
and she

never likes my anything.

No WTF or OMG—
current approval
of thoughts in my head,
of gems from my days.

She never smilies my life.

(no title)

Someday
I'll think back
wistfully

to the day

I wrote about
being
nostalgic.

of   hearth   and   home

Lightning Bugs

In the dark, they would flicker fluorescent—
Yellow, green, gold, elusive, and magic.
The off-again, on-again wink-wink-winking of Kentucky June.

Iridescent balloons round our eyes,
bubbles from the bushes, from the fields, from the grasses,
lighter than Puck-like dandelion puffs,
blink-blink-blinking
in 3-D air.

Cartoon creatures, drifting through dusk, they would pull at us—
we weathercocks, inebriated , as we ran in sweat,
with our gravel-patch knees and skinny-bone legs.

And if the day had been heavy, as it could be, back then,
if our little livers had been squashed, our visions wrung dry,
in circles and back, we would fly with them, high,
from worlds afar to electric lights and home.

And almost as if I'd known I'd remember—
from a city far away; from concrete and scrapers,
far after the dusk of my deep southern sky—
my warm southern womb,

lightning bugs, floating at random in a summer night's dream,
in a wave of remembering, illuminate, still, the darkness of my road.

Jewish Christmas—Buffalo, New York

The neighbors would invite us to see their tree.
Mom and Dad would consent, though they watched
from the window as we left. Bundled in muffs, scarves,
mittens, four Jewish girls would journey far
through snow and cultures, to the house next door.

Tinsel and gold, green and stuffed stockings,
sparkles and lights, white feathered angels—
all around us aromas of Unholy Gods.

How hard to look on, through timid, young eyes.
How hard to walk home, convictions in place,
loaded down with beliefs, candy-cane melting
in the sweat of small palms.

Remember This

In Mrs. Tingue's First Grade class,
I fell in love with Timmy. I remember
orange electric air, prickles of heat on my cheeks.
My mother smiled, said—puppy love,
when on cooling concrete steps I confessed.
The Kentucky sun warmly grasped our necks.

I was insulted. How belittling her smile.
And I remember thinking—remember
this day, this feeling, this slight,
though I didn't even know that word.

First Grade love—a surprise gift in ribbons.
You don't even know its name.
Just a poke here and there
a twitch in a paper-bagged lunch.

And I remember vowing—remember this,
same exact feeling
not to be waved away by adults.
Experience, their only advantage.

One day, Timmy, in the back of class,
next to Dixie-cupped lima bean seedlings,
asked if I knew what a Playboy was,
—a naked girl, he answered himself and ran off.

And I remember, sideswiped and red,
my balance shoved off its heels.
Naked girl? Naked girl?
And I swirled down the drain
as if fever-filled,
what is this? What is this?
With no reference to guide,
and still fighting defeat,
spiraling into
Remember this. Remember this.

And I have remembered that.

Stealing Pink Lipstick

Jill Kaplan made me wild. Introduced irreverence.
We would jump to the sky on her bed, never fell, never broke
it or our arms or our bony stick-legs.

We had plans. Singing at volumes obscene,
and bouncing on her quilted bed- tambourines flailing,
no harmony or solos; unison. We knew Ed Sullivan
would call to us, send scouts to convince us to honor
his stage. And her Mom made grilled cheese in the kitchen.

We were pharmacy spies. Jill knew the cashier was KGB and
we snuck in the aisles round cough syrups on sale,
writing in note pads we hid in our mittens. Unhappy cashier.

Before the first dance, at the YMCA, one of many
my parents feared—being foreign—
before that dance, at the Five-and-Ten, before I even knew,
she swiped a barrette, for the dance, for a lark and then

this rose pink lipstick that I liked as I touched
its cold metal case, found its way from the shelf
to my hand to my pocket
and out.

And at the dance that my parents were very afraid of,
at the dance where obviously nobody asked us,
even though I knew I could move and dance
as with Jill on her bed. I was so so dying to dance.

And the stolen pink lipstick, I put on in the girls' room
and then hid in my coat when Jill's mom picked us up—
which later I was too scared, too ashamed,
to wear it or to hold it, cold metal case, again.

But now when I push myself into the danger,
when the line waves ahead like a scarlet bandana,
I am holding that lipstick, smooth and cold,
I am cracking that bed till it almost breaks,
and Jill Kaplan jumps, jubilant, by my side.

Ghost of Thanksgiving Past

The snow pats on my window, then
falls into place on the ground as
we all, once again, fall back into
schedules, appointments, studies...

Vacation is over and bits of
not-so-exciting bread
leave reminders of feasts;
cranberry, squash and pumpkins that turned
into cars and buses once the clock struck
Sunday evening.

Snow patting drizzle lulls me to sleep
as books and papers remind that it's time
to settle down.

How pale these papers
compared to the faces of friends.

Piano at Night

It's funny she thought that I'd have lots of sugar.
She passed through my doorway, a cup in her hand,
for a cake she was baking for guests from abroad.
And knowing my unstocked cupboards well,
I began to collect from various bowls
found randomly in my kitchen.
One on the table, and one on the shelf—
crystallized crumbs here and there—
Three-fourths of a cup, a bit lumpy and brown
from coffee spoons hastily used.
Why would she think that I have sugar?
No aromas exude from my door.
No cinnamon spice or nutmeg delights
float from my window sills to hers.
And she took the sweet mixture, though not all
she'd expected, downstairs to prepare for those coming.
Perhaps it was the sound of piano at night
or dance on my terrace that misled her.

Spin and Sing

I
Sleeping
soft
on your belly.
A muffin.
Hands raised like daisies
across blue blanket.
Dolphin smile—curled up at the sides.
So still at night my ears strain to
hear you still
breathing—(butterfly) sighs,
sucking and sighs
drunk with sleep.

II
Signs of a modern baby.
Throw-away diapers and head guards.
Soapless shampoo and electric bottle warmers.
Mobiles that spin and sing, spin and sing...

III
My grandmother had no refrigerator
to keep her baby's milk.
No nursing bras or washing machine.
No pre-strained fruits or pre-chewed meats.
In the kitchen, I prepare your formula.
Sad empty breasts
tire in the night,
return to their
other role.

IV
In the bedroom your father stares
at the ceiling, thinking about a friend
who had an affair in Vienna.
I bring you your bottle and then join him.
He wonders if we'll make love tonight.

Overwhelming Wonder

When Oren sleeps
he dreams of golden lions
that he battles with sticks
he's collected from the yard.
And in the darkness of his room
his yellow night-light shines—
big eared bunny with
a blue bugle.
Sometimes the lion runs away
leaving Oren triumphant on a
hill of victory.
Sometimes it advances,
pushing Oren from his bed,
shaking
through thick darkness
into my unlit room
into my white arms,
which tremble
in overwhelming
wonder.

Trip to the Theatre

You sat on my knees
like dry firewood
stiff and ignitable,
matchbox boy
your tiny tendons
turned kindling
taut, tight
ready for flight.
Antipodal Pinocchio
your heart like
a jumping bean
hopped in the dark
and hardened
with each start,
eyes inflamed,
concentration acute,
like an arrow—
bow pulled
and waiting.

At the Airport

The day before arrival is best—
return departure countdown
not yet begun.
And on the day of our meeting
I clothe my babes in
velvet and white lace—
North American packages
lavished
from grandparents abroad.

They look like *Hutz La'aretz*—
those kids.
An ode to their roots,
all cleaned and rich—
their *Sabra* prickles hide
in leafy fabrics from afar.

On the way, aware
that time has passed, I'm anxious
of changes to come through the gates—
more grey, or less hair,
less tall, or more round,
less patience, more caution—
no phone call can train for such turns.

And as the grandparents approach
half-run and half-hobble
in their regard,
not quite hidden from me—
the surprise of
my age
in their eyes.

Hutz La'aretz— Hebrew, literally: "outside the country";
used for abroad or, in this context, foreign

Sabra— Hebrew, literally the prickly pear cactus or its
fruit, but an idiom for native Israelis (prickly on the
outside, soft and sweet inside, like the fruit)

Commitment

Erev Yom Kippur, Ramat-Gan

—Just listen to the quiet,
I say to my young daughter as
I pull her to the terrace
after the pre-fast meal.
—Just listen to the quiet.
You won't find quiet like that
out of Israel—in any city—
quiet like that.

—Stop it *Ima*, she answers to
the words I have aimed at her,
as she adjusts her helmet straps.
A day of no cars and only bikes,
you must commit to atonement on
Israeli streets. Soul searching
on wheels, not so easy.

America.
Driving to *Shul*
on a rainy weeknight
past malls and plazas and
not-to-be-entered ice cream parlors
bursting with whipped toppings.
My sisters and I miss
too much school,
the teacher says.

A full day of prayer is
too long in Ramat Gan.
We compromise on just *Ne'ilah*.
Walking to *Shul*, I hold her hand
and wonder if she'll set a table,
white and broad, of her own one day,
graced with pomegranates and wine.

Ima— Hebrew, Mother

Ne'ilah— Hebrew, the closing prayer service at the end of
Yom Kippur, the Day of Atonement

Shul— Hebrew: Synagogue

Big Kids

Big kids don't make ashtrays from clay,
with fat, clumsy hands.
Big kids don't put on plays in the living room,
using scarves and lipsticks
they've found in your drawers.
They don't dance,
arms out, in the yard,
as they sing in strange voices
at volumes untamed.

Big kids will tell you maybe
part of a story, or part of a part.
They will pass you in halls,
sit beside you on the couch
and think they've divulged—
little crumbs of their privacy—particles
you catch with your eyebrow plucker.

They'll take your car,
they'll finish the milk,
they'll point out your faults
and echo your fears.

And then one strange day,
you had imagined as far away,
they'll pack their lives,

leaving

ashtrays and songs,
living rooms and lipsticks,
scarves all unbothered and arranged
in your orderly,
untouched, drawers.

Paris Unsaid

I sent my boys off to Paris today.
Twenty-two and twenty,
the same age as I,
when captured by
the Seine's rainbow twinkle,
Élysée's grandeur.

They are cynically young, from
press keys and wires,
with gadgets literally
out of their ears.

They will turn the same corners,
eat the same bread;
their boundless dreams,
though well-hidden,
as green as mine at that time.
Anxiously I wait to see how they fared
away from their text-message world.

Will they feel autumn slide through
the narrow back alleys?
Will they smell lovers' sighs in small dim cafes?
Will their sneakered feet remember
the cobblestone, worn and uneven
from horses past and sports cars present?

Will they tell of glances and blushing
and wet autumn leaves and cool white marble,
of ponds, round and shallow with toy boats that float
as children jump past with their plaid woven scarves and
their small yapping dogs?

I have walked them to school—
these two young men.
I have taught them to swim and to drive.
But I can't help but wonder and worry a bit—
have I taught them to hear what's unsaid?

Note to Grown Kid

Inspired by "This Is Just to Say" by William Carlos Williams

I parked your red car
across the street under
the tree that sheds.

Your sister was thrilled to drive
in your absence and hopes that
you bought her that orange hat.

Please resume your turn
with the doggy—his paws
miss the wet of the leaves.

Fresh milk in the fridge
for your plump raisin cornflakes—neither
of which ran out for the week.

My computer is out. Again.
Can you check it? Had no one
to help, roll their eyes, or sigh.

You'll have to catch up on
our TV series. Tried to hold out
but was bored. Sorry.

Leave wash on the counter, find
keys on your desk, your mail's
on the kitchen table.

Hope flight was good. Peek
in but don't wake us.
I'll know.

of   that   which   is   around

The Field

Lexington, Kentucky, 1961

Kentucky—green grass so blue it confuses,
so tall, we can hide
sitting straight or
slithering as snakes on our
bellies browned from the ground.
The field is vast and the grass
is so blue and so fresh
that it reaches inside us, we friends
of the meadow. We meet to expand,
we meet to escape in blue grass
on our backs looking upwards,
past tall reeds to castles,
to seas, upwards and on beyond blue grass
and then.

American Tu B'Shvat—Nuts

Sometime mid-February
our Sunday School Principal
would walk into class behind

a box filled with bags.
"The Celebration for Trees!"
she would stoutly announce.

On Jewish walls, posters
of brown-skinned children
with *Tembel* hats
would look out at us,
in our warm winter wraps,
in our white Western skin.

To each of us a bag:
one walnut, two almonds,
eight raisins and carob—
all hard as our heavy history books.

How we pitied those children
in *Eretz Yisrael*.
How we thought of them
rejoicing over stale fruit
and nuts
in the middle
of winter.

Tu B'Shvat— Hebrew, the fifteenth of the Hebrew month,
Shvat, celebrated as the birthday / new year of the trees

Tembel— Hebrew, a domed hat, symbolic of the Israeli
pioneer-farmers

Eretz Yisrael— Hebrew, literally, the land of Israel,
meaning the actual place

Tumbling After—Jack and Jill

rolling on ground
knotted and gnarled
this mound
like the back of a toad
from tree roots protruding
being bumped on green-brown,
brown-green on spotted hills
earth-rock knobs, all green-brown,
brown-green, and black
and down.

Israeli Fall

I am unfamiliar still
with the ways of this season.
Having parched all summer, dizzy with heat,
only ants remain steady in their convoy.
Endlessly they appear on my counter,
undaunted by soapy sponges, which
dry out in seconds.

From time to time some
air slides in between layers
of brown-white heat—
a whiff of pomegranate
or juicy wine seeds—
and then, again, heat.

This season is ambivalent—
now promising, now dry.

Edgy with uncertainty
I await the distinct touch of
Winter's wet paws.

Tel Aviv Beach—Winter Abundance

On the rocks near the beach
a splintered sky—
grey-boned and cracked,
a wide, bolted crack—
white sun
like soup pours evenly.
Out here
I am next to
pebbles and peddlers
chalky sand on bare knuckles
tight winter air
and the push of the water
and the rich salt of kelp
fatly green in the tide—
the cool and the warmth,
the sky and the sea
exulting in
winter abundance.

Reduction of the Day

From thin soup light
to thickening evening,
the day evaporates slowly,
lidless,
into the night.

Spring Forward

The hunchbacked old lady collects that dark extra hour from the worn winter sky. And left in its place—the promise of firsts and of greening spring and then hot summer mist—in her burlap bag, next to apples and twigs, it will rest until winter, when she'll pull it out and place it, once more, with regret, in an unreceptive sky still clinging to the light.

Stray Cries

Tel Aviv

i
The cats here are pointed—
these Mid-Eastern strays that
wander nomadic past trashcans and motorbikes.
All Winter long they have hidden,
and curled, coming up only
to stretch out their bodies on
steamy hoods of Renaults and Fiats.
They are covered bones walking
bent leg, swollen heads,
not the fat fat-cats
of my American past.
They're Egyptian and sphinx-like,
with slanted cheeks and
eye-liner slits. They slink and slide
between poles and in stink
of urban stairwells,
in niches they find in
yellowing concrete,
their mewling on mute
for the season.

ii
And then in the Spring,
my windows open again,
I hear in the night all
their growls and hisses,
their high pitched mooing.
They scurry and bellow below.

I sometimes think of them
newly born, flexing their lungs,
jaws open wide, teeny teeth glowing,
those mischievous siblings
nestled near mothers—they cry
simply to announce their arrival.

iii
But tonight's cries are
eerie–desperately sharp
cries to the trees, to
deceptive warm air,
to an unresponsive moon
that shines too brightly
on my white sheets.
And as I listen, I, too, will toss,
stretching out, in alliance
to the moon, to the stars and
Egyptian strays.

Hannah

"Rare Sumatran Tiger Eats Her Cubs at the Biblical Zoo"

is what the headline says and before getting all
she didn't want babes who were born under lock—

know that it happens in the wild, too. They sometimes go all

Cannibal Mom, eat off their cubs' cabbage heads,
then leave their limp bodies, sprawled, runny eggs
in the grasses.

This one had done it three times before—the neglect, that is,
not the eating. Hannah had a history of not taking care, three times,
her endangered pups endangered, the Zoo had stepped in to help.

But she ate them this time, after
six weeks of grooming and pruning and care,
after six weeks of tar teats cracked and tugged,
brittle. Six weeks. They thought she was good this time.

(Only 400 more on the Isle of Sumatra and 400 more left in zoos.)

The stories our minds will produce
to make sense of this worst of all possible crimes.

A babe in a bucket, a child in a bag,
cut up and dismembered,
thrown to the hills.

What is it that pinches her nerves till they squeak,
that rids her of instinct inherent?
What is it that throws her at panic's wall?

the incessant need? the yowls? the whining?
The terror of tending the tender?

Or maybe it's nothing.
No rhyme no reason.
No time that is better
or worse. Just snap.

Tel Aviv Love Song

This Tel Aviv city, on disappeared dunes.
Pushing, pulsing and salty sea.
This urban safari, this basket of nations,
unrelated patches next to blue waves.
Where once yellow-white
blended pure on your palette,
now ashen soot on your peeling facades.
For years I wandered your streets in disdain.
You Bauhaus white city of falling structures,
you neglected metropolis of poorly planned hopes,
I did not learn to love you, Tel Aviv.

And then something changed.
Perhaps it's the years, my acceptance of wear
or maybe a loosening of shoulds and why-nots,
I can see you more clearly today.

I can see your small workshops of
grease, wood and metal, your baskets of
rice, coriander and cumin,
twisting pathways, alleys
and all of it covered in a dust of light sand.
I can see silver scrapers jut out to the sky,
fancy ladies, big hats, folded homeless, tattered mats.

A city, like any—like Paris, Madrid,
a city like any, like no other city—
a Jew in front and a Jew behind,
Arabs, foreign workers all longing for home.
Magnificent weave of woes and wealths.
I sing your praise, repent disregard.

My feet in sand footprints of those gone ahead,
I study your face as if it weren't mine,
as if you belonged to somebody else,
as a guest in a stranger's backyard.

Winter Cleaning / 'Til It's Spring

Let me squeeze the freeze right out of you.
Let me wring your dirty kerchief clouds
and drain your skies of grey and burn.
Let me scrub till there's no white on your collar,
no rust round your ring, no sludge in your tub.
'Til the steam from your halted
earth cookings is still,
'til the count of your ice-burdened
willows is nil.
Shards that are draped on the line, I will basket
and set near the fire to fade.

Tired of finger-tipped pirate hooks,
of peg legs lost in thermal boots,
of tossing on seas of choppy soaps.

Let me bleach your white drifts 'til
the rabbit's uncovered,
'til my soil-soiled knuckles are bleeding.
Let me swab your bare trees.
Let me scour your lakes,
frozen hills, sleeping streams,
'til Spring.

of loves

Captured Lights—Who is your love?

she asks as we walk arm in arm
down the Seine.
My thoughts are of orange and pink sky
when I turn to her.
Straw hat, cheeks rosy-purple,
and her mandarin hair
reflects the light—teasing
nearby painters and poets, it says:
"They're mine. I have captured the fleeting lights!"

—Your love? She reminds.
Her words find and fill niches
between pastels
bringing pictures
of mothers and sisters,
lovers, and you're my love, you're
waiting for letters, clippings
hotel napkins.
Her arm is strong, graceful.

—You are. I answer.
I silently sink back
into orange and pink.

Buffalo Romance

1.
Past loves declared
over sweet summer teas,
sit polished and full
on your Formica table,
beside the kettle.
Like old witches
who sell apples,
we drew each one out
with care.

Now we are clean.

2.
In the Fall, I notice
our awning in the attic.
We never hung plants on its bare poles.
Fat rain drips from them slowly
as I write to say how
things are. Below,
the garden's earth grows muddy
and I haven't yet
brought in the squash.
A plane breaks through the clouds.
I feel like you're on it.

Just now, leaving me.

3.
That night after the city's first snowfall
your saxophone sang those
thick, slow notes
as I walked by your apartment.
A yellow light from inside
mixed with shadows on your face
as I watched through the elms.
Before, the gray-white snow
had seemed in place,
until I stood there
remembering
the color of the leaves

when I last heard you play.

Whirlpool

For Shani

She does this thing with
her eyes
as she puts on
her play for me in
the living room.

She rolls them up and backwards
not looking at
yet talking to
me all the time.

Her four year old face
is angled and square
knowing more now than I
could ever have known.

Floating about the room,
her skin bears my wounds
like jewels,
her silk-maize locks,
and my fear,
her tiara.

In another dimension
I know she's my mother
or husband who left—
she and I
together
here turning
on a whirlpool carpet
both of our eyes
rolled up and backwards
in protest.

Fur

In the dark,
between your chest and your shoulder,
I find that hollow,
that concave place
concealed and covered by
fur.

Like a rabbit,
I burrow my head
enjoying the velvet soft
of this very
private niche.

Today, male models will wax
their bodies clean like David's.
But I savor
the luxury, thick
across your chest.

Minor Misunderstanding

She says,
Even though he is
rancorous and rude,
insensitive and crude,
I know that he loves me
because he drapes his arm gently
round my waist as we sleep
after an evening bout
of argument.

He says,
Even though she's stopped
talking, her words hit like hammers
and nothing will change.
I am trapped and have no
recollection of contact at night.

Unaware

The nape of your neck
the slender of your wrists
tempt me,
enticing with their
elegance and strength.
I long to touch
their tender darkness
in the middle of the day.
The parts of you I
love best
unaware of the stirring
they create.

For Years This Is True

You go to sleep before me.
For years, this is true.
I slip into warmth, white sheets
you've pre-baked
like loaves in an oven for me.
For years, this is true.

I've seen your arms strong holding babes,
holding parents. I've seen your legs gone,
wrapped around other limbs and
come back. Your back
has been arched, your back has been bent,
your feet have been by mine for years.
So strange, the night,
when I slide by your side, join a world
you have already entered.

For years this is true,
and I know of our comfort,
for you're here in our bed,
toasting sheets, dampening
pillows with heat.
Endurance, the crown of our love.

For years this is us,
comfy in quilts and flannel.
For now you sleep quiet,
deep in the dark.
But by low light of stars,
barely seen
on your soft old face,
on your old soft lips,
with me unable to quench,
lies a whisper which aches
for surprise.

Right Before

Right before the rain pelts, when the sky is still
dry like a glass that's been wiped with a paper towel,
squeaky, yet clouds hang like teats before feeding.

Right before the cat goes for the leaf that's
been twitching, his tense behind jerking, in time
side to side as foreplay before his leap.

Right before the coffee is sipped by the lips and rolls
on the tongue, when the nose has already been filled
with the brown of the beans and their slow, dark roast.

Right before the violin cracks in the hall and the maestro,
with sweat on his brow, is positioned, arm up with his bow
on your mark, get set, ready....!

Right before I know where you live, what you do,
when you're not yet unwrapped, a new face at a dinner,
a smile on a bus, a frequency airwave of only those ions which

race through space, bumping walls, thumping skin,
unidentified, nameless, the thrill of not knowing, uncertain,
just barely, but knowing and all, right before.

Barely

There's a lot of quiet in this room.
Open a window and air it out.
Spray a few words to leave a scent.
Steam some music over a blue-yellow flame.

There's a lot of quiet in this room.
Let it expand within the walls.
Stretch it like a cat on a woven rug.
Squeeze in between it like sheets on a bed.

Let it breathe.
Lock the doors and shut the shades.
Let it fill
ceiling to floor,
the drains, the sockets,
the faucets and keyholes.

We're stuffed in here,
our shoulders squashed
side by side. We're pumpkins
ready to burst,
silent seeds
in tight orange air.

And there's barely room for you and me.
So very much quiet between so few.
So very much quiet between just two.

Remote Control

It's a nice game we have going
here. Buttons are pressed.
Reactions achieved. I play
the dog to your Pavlov.

And I know that's the story.
I could stop if I tried.
Could stop salivating,
not hear all those bells.

But I so love your face
when you're pleased
with yourself. When you
think I don't see, that it's

all undetected.
Ignorance
of your moves,
I pretend.

A Certain Risk

If I say we're
losing touch
you are pressed and
there's the risk of us
losing touch.

If I say nothing about
losing touch
we continue like this and
there's the risk of us
losing touch.

Reconciliation

And here is the poem of
our reconciliation.
A moon. It should have a moon.
Purple lighthouse on a pier
and a moon pulling waves
pulling shoreless waves back to shore.

Did we have a moon
before we parted?
Was it a moon that
we missed before
reuniting?

The warmth of our bodies
under blankets in bed.
The soft heat of your breath
upon my drawn lashes.
The damp of our sleep-heavy
sweat on the pillows.
And our limbs like vines
intertwined,
leaving no need for
lighthouses
or waves or moons.

The Sweetness in Longing

There's a sweetness in longing,

an undertone ripple—
the jasmine of ache,
a residual lightness
that makes it ok,
worth feeling, enduring.

As if there's a choice

past the unfocused gaze
the unnoticed air

past the sky out the window
the breath rising slow.

There's a sweetness in longing,

like the fragrance of evening,
that softens the wrongs,
makes the waiting worth waiting,
the memory worth remembering,
a fine undercurrent that flows, that holds,
right beneath the sigh

steady and strong and
just sweet enough
to sustain the pain.

of   transitions

Entitlement and Myths about Pink Cotton Panties

She wears those black lace panties now.
Not pink cotton ones from the supermarket
next to yellow plastic gloves and Oreos.

They're satin, opaque and devilishly rich—
the swoop of their fall envelopes her curves
like water over hills, green with the wet of moss.

In high school, warnings of an envisioned accident,
being rushed off—ambulance, doctors—
her panties torn or stained.

And a locker-room side-glance unveiled those few girls
who donned frilly undies and laughed, heads brazenly up
in the heat of the showers.

Poor misled girls whose mothers didn't
know or guide in the self-respect
of pink cotton panties.

You have character. They said. You shine like a flower
in a room of people—your wit, your humor and honesty.
And pink cotton panties.

And she didn't yet know that her mother had brassieres
from mail-order catalogues, or that the touch of a breast
could bring pain or peace or a surge of breath that reaches past clouds.

But she wears those black lace panties now, allowing extravagance
of hand-washable fabrics, claiming her shape, her God-given turns
and their lure.

The line of her cleavage, the round of her belly,
the untold power intrinsic in her being,
the rest of her sum.

In the Flaw

There was a softness in seeing her
wearing glasses
instead of the contact lenses
she normally wore.
She seemed less
perfect, less
constricted by norms
of beauty. More relaxed and imperfect.
Slightly flawed. Slightly unbuttoned.
Flawed just enough to make her human.
Approachable.

Too much order
makes for nervousness.

To disturb that fine order,
to shake it up like you do with your hair
when you towel it dry and then
rabble-rouse it rough with havoc-crazed fingers.
Like sweeping off the setting of a perfect table
with the widest swoop of
one reckless arm.
So beautiful—upside down,
just the crash
of glass shattering pieces.

Or maybe just the stain
from the bottom of a wineglass
purple on white
of a starched,
ironed cloth.

Perfection has its problems.
Release is in the flaw.

Noticed

I noticed her hand first,
grasped round the pole of the bus as she stood.
There was nothing extravagant going on there—
only big. Large wrist, not fat, just big.
Thick fingers that could never fit into
slender white gloves of Spring.
But they stood out just the same, like
a peach in her throat or razor boar bristles
peeking out powdered skin.
So different it was, the hand.
Her fingers held lightly as the road tossed its turns,
through gentrified streets
made anew.

In a navy blue pants suit, softly pressed and her hair
long, black and straightened, or a wig.
And she noticed me notice and in response to her flush,
her restrained annoyance,
my eyes darted downward and stumbled
onto the size of her shoes—
small heals and simple, and
just as big. And I wanted to say
—You be who you are!

But that is so stupid and condescending,
and I didn't know where
to set my eyes. In the window's reflection,
I saw her, I saw me and I lowered my head
for having noticed or paid
any attention at all.

Eliyahu in the Skies

And Eliyahu has left this world
from the hospice, left pain and
the old bearded woman who eats
all the sugar, dining
from her wheelchair
in the hall with all
other wheel-chaired people,
waiting for lunch.

"Ay *Ima*. Ay *Ima*," you called.
We didn't know if you
were craving your mother or if
those sounds escaped in pain,
in futility. Random.

Even then you were leaving
us back and forth from
the bed to Morocco,
from the pain to the skies,
from your unshaven face
to your big sister's kitchen
with honey-covered pastries,
jokes and laughs, stories
only you and your
siblings understood.

Eliyahu set free.
Have you found your *Ima*?
Have you claimed your cakes?
Does your *Ima* sit by you,
wiping your brow as she
sings you to sleep?

Ima— Hebrew, Mother

Israelite Woman Leaving Egypt

I remember giving in to those flat beige breads.
"Faster woman, it's time to move on."
The proportions were wrong. How much water?
How much flour? This dough, so runny,
dripping through my fingers like soured milk.
Wrist-deep I wade through the mixture in need
of bread that is slow and full.
More water? More flour?

I miss my Egyptian neighbor,
who is such a good cook.
I'm in need of her laugh,
her ease with a mortar.
But she mourns over curls
of her firstborn son,
and as mine looks on,
I am ashamed
to be baking.

Wish of the Bereaved, Memorial Day Ceremony, Tel Aviv

Just not to be sitting here,
in the first few rows.
To be on the side, or in back,
on stage—reciting a poem,

even

calling the names.

Just not
to be sitting
here.

To feel the pain, yet remain indebted to
that distant soldier to whom I am grateful.
The luxury of gratefulness, like a
drop of brine for the void of my mouth.

To feel a part,
but not my

entire.

To mourn lost courage

but not your voice,

the stench of your sweat,
the bite of your eye,
an unused pillow, an orderly room,

finality

that never ends.

Watching

For VeeVee 1974

The summer wind flutters gently through the palms.
A soft, moth-winged wind beats almost
unnoticed through the palms.
And from the window, VeeVee,
in her pajamas, sits watching.
Everyone else sleeps.

From the mountain, down to the valley,
sequined windows turn out one by one.
Like the subtle blinking of eyes they nod off to sleep
'til only one across the street, one behind the trees

remains.

A sky-grown lily-melon moon
ripe with summer satisfaction
at home amidst the
plump of the streetlights—

reassuring sleepless VeeVee of her uncertain future,
dipping behind shingled roofs and clothes lines,
drifting slowly, slowly to distant palms, her moon,
melting with stars, lights and sleep.

Watching for VeeVee II—Gulf War

Our nightly phone call—
Your dream still occurs:
sudden siren, futile fumbling for
boxes in closets.
A mask for your child
and no knowledge of its use.

Numbness.

Was that really us?
I'm amazed as I listen.
As Yanks turned Israeli,
it couldn't be so.
My stick-like sister,
I would laugh at you and then.

Your red-haired crest
crowning your head, cock-eyed.
Burrs on your leggings and
high-top red shoes—we'd
chase you and say
the Green Booga would
get you, and you ran,
skinny bones.

I wrote you sweet poems.

This is not really us—
having been through a war.
Having been under fire
in London or Warsaw.
This is not really us—we sisters in safety.
And our colors don't fit—
hazel eyes, orange curl

not

black and white prints from
an album or archive.
On the phone, I am silent,
though wanting to speak.
Sorry, I can't laugh
at your red-haired crest
or your high-top red shoes,
or the burrs on your leggings.
Sorry for Green Boogas and
sirens and masks, and I pray
you won't leave
me in fear
alone.

In Waiting—Israeli Unrest

In a plastic baggie,
the best of my rings,
stuffed on the side
of my dresser drawer,
with a few crumpled dollars
and thyroid meds,

just in case.

Organized tins of sardines,
stuffed grape leaves.
Bottles of spring water, olive oil.
You would think—for a feast
on Jerusalem hills,
with a blanket spread gracious
on poppy-filled fields.

What will I do when
the siren sounds?
What will I grab in that
moment of

now?

Purple sneakers
in waiting,
my days my nights
in suspense.
Remember this tomato.
Breathe in this peach.

What can I plan for when
the siren sounds?
When I run for my kidneys,
I run for my breath, before
the roof, the plaster, my legs

fall down.

The land of milk and honey.
No Polish village or Russian farm.

Yet here it is,
still on my arm,
too familiar.

Un-tattooed in purple,
it covers my skin in
unseen ink from

pasts
that continually

repeat.

Yet In Sight

1.
Can we throw this out? He asks
me, impatient with what
he sees as clutter—a bowl,
in a cupboard overflowing.
Throwing it out helps unburden
his spirit, aids him to climb
from the overfilled pit
that is his day.

Just leave it, I try.
It's not bothering you—
I use it for candy,
once a year, every year—
a tradition, a totem I've kept
for our children and theirs—
a symbol, an heirloom, a passage
of time, a memory still
in the making.

2.
I personify things.
Some of value, some not.
They speak to me even
when they are unseen,
the thought of them gone—
like an aunt or an uncle, a cousin
with whom I watched clouds on my back,
with whom I ate fruit from my grandmother's yard,
and then passed them on,
over to you.

A memory hoarder,
the bowl is a crumb—
a chained pocket watch, a locket,
a broach, a whiff from a kitchen
of smells long away.

3.
So silly, that bowl.
It's no big deal.
Put it back in its place,
with the candlesticks, vases
and lace tablecloths—

to appear once a year,
on a specific day—
an attempt to remain
yet in sight.

Dance of the Returning Children

When they leave,
it tugs at first.
You are nauseous,
slightly. Irritable.

Irritable insides.
Is that a syndrome?
Or something ignored,
pushed to denial.

De Nile.
That river in Egypt where we focus
on palm trees and camels, on women
washing clothes with wet stones.

We wash away
thoughts about this
about that and our
soon to be ending future 'til

they return again.
Fill the space with oasis,
their light and their strength,
their confusion. Then leave.

With their laughter and anger,
their plans and their hopes hanging
out of their bags like left-behind
sweatshirts and socks.

And the dance continues,
back and forth, back and forth,
a dizzying waltz,
'til they're ready at last—

leaving
you and me
to find our own feet,
redefine the way

we move in,
we move out
and around
each other again.

Pockets

In the folds of my pockets I find notes.
In my jackets, my pants, my worn winter coats.

     sour cream, shampoo, 2% milk, cranberries, Aunt Anne, gravy

Found long after, with a ball of moist lint,
stick of gum, a tissue, a dime turning lime.

     3 sweet potatoes, ginger, green tea, 2 leeks, shoe polish, poem, tooth

Seasons pass, reappear and they're there, in hiding, crumpled,
stained and torn. Their contents reflecting their time.

     Blue Moon lyrics, rye bread, fat rain, flea collar, Oh anemone!

Momentary wisps of winters gone, recipes past,
words or beloveds in need of a visit.
Each list has its meanings, its flavors, its scents.
In days of bananas, of music, of mint,

of people I cooked for or tables I set.
Words that I ran with or notes that I sang,
tearless shampoos for soft baby heads,
soles worn from worry in need of repair.

Did I visit that cousin, that poem, that pie?
Did I learn the words to that song?

Long are the lists of missions completed.
Long are the lists of those that were not.

I revisit those lists, faded days, vanished years.
I, like my pockets, can't seem to let go.

Celia Merlin

On a slow afternoon, one where goals pass achievements,
I Google my name, Celia Merlin, and then
up pop some YouTubes,
and a mention or two of this and of that. And then
"Celia Merlin,"
the one long gone, pops up,
on a gravestone—
in front of my face—Celia Merlin—
the one after whom I was named.

Who took that picture—"Dearest Mom" on that gravestone?
An agency trying to pull me past, dangling
Birth, Marriage, Death
with papers and proof—
dates deemed important, but not.

What I know—
She was Russian. She came to the States,
changed her name and worked hard,
had two boys, lost her husband,
and left. Joined her brother in the desert—
the Jewish desert, with her two *Americanshkeh* boys.
I've been told she was strict, pulled their ears when they strayed,
and worked hard and could probably be found in
a Philip Roth novel or Malamud short story, and
was hard and could cook.

But I never tasted your steamy stuffed cabbage
or sat on a stool by your side.
I've never laughed, argued, yelled
or cried in Yiddish at your
blistered hands and life. Never echoed
your accent or funny translations and the
velvet candy box with your unsugared photos
is easily closed, put aside, dismissed.
Your pictures send no invitation.

To be named after one I never met—
"Dearest Mom" looms across the screen
in stone, an absent connection.

Ships

> *"..so on the ocean of life, we pass..."*
> —*Henry Wadsworth Longfellow*

We sit in the mall café
talking photographs.
The air is plastic,
the music benign.

In a booth near the restroom,
holding tall ice coffees,
you say you'll be leaving again.
And I know.

In your photos, purple feathers,
headdresses of Kings,
fat crocodile teeth,
plush carpets of pines.

There are women with weavings,
brown children on boats,
angles of blue and
the rust of red soil.

I am losing my breath.
I am nauseous with awe.
I am inside the lens
of your eye.

There are shadows of green,
spreading fingers on rocks, and
Einstein-like webs
in the trees.

I am covered with waves.
I am licking a cloud.
I am climbing a
steeple of slate.

—Is there anything else..?
        the waitress asks.
-No, thanks.
        We pack up and leave.

Each to the corners
we've picked for ourselves.

You to your knapsack,
your travel-worn boots.
Me to my words
and the mall.

For A Second

In the middle of the city
I smell a charcoal grill

see mustard, ketchup, and green toad relish.

And for just that second
I feel the sun

think of blue green grass

see my mother's bare shoulders
over her polka dot strapless

and I'm hiding
on a branch in a willow

where I hear adult
laughter and silliness

see a picnic cloth flap

taste bad lemonade

and look for my sisters
spread out on the lawn

and cover my knees that
are scratched from the climbing

and I gather the sun as
it sets on our heads

and collect the mustard
the ketchup and all

to take home. But just
for that second.

In Return

You get soft perfect skin
and I get your chair,
I told my niece who had found
a seat at the crowded party.

For the very first time,
I offered my age
in return
for indulgence.

Her hand held a plate of
creamy white cakes
and, in the other, some
sparkling pink wine.

Glittering, she looked, and I
looked at her skin like a rose.
She rose, nodded, and acquiesced.

A chair
for your
aging aunt
in return
for soft
perfect skin—

the better deal by far.

Ozymandias Revisited

after the sonnet by Percy Bysshe Shelley

No one will write a book of my life.
Or a script for a movie, a score for a play.
No Wikipedia will journal my trail, early life and career.
No one will uncover the secrets I take, no aunts will fill gaps
in the me that you knew. And if they do, soon enough they will fade
and evade with the days that flew.

My name will pass on, as Celine or Celeste or Emma Sophia.
And my recipes will be known as
"Sophie's Soufflé" or "Sadie's Sage Chicken,"
with no scent of me in the rising steam.

No works will be found in my dresser or laptop
before they are given or tossed in the street.

I am no Winston Churchill, Galileo Galilei.
I have built no bridges or composed fat concertos that
may lengthen my stay for a spell.

I'm the man at the counter, the girl at the dance,
the kid with the baseball, the guy with the truck.
I will not be remembered for good or bad luck.

I am me I am you,
with the wave of a hand,
the whiff of a breath,
like the flight of a leaf,
I am gone.

www.ingramcontent.com/pod-product-compliance
Lightning Source LLC
Chambersburg PA
CBHW050743180726
48003CB00019B/847